W9-DHV-699

J. T. Snow

by Mark Stewart

ACKNOWLEDGMENTS

The editors wish to thank J. T. Snow for his cooperation in preparing this book.
Thanks also to Integrated Sports International for their assistance.

PHOTO CREDITS

All photos courtesy AP/Wide World Photos, Inc. except the following:

Michael Zito/Sports Chrome – Cover, 4 center right
V. J. Lovero/California Angels – 5 center right, 6, 25 bottom, 26, 28, 29, 31, 42, 47
John Cordes/California Angels – 4 bottom right, 5 bottom right, 8, 30, 33, 34, 37
Kirk Schlea/California Angels – 39 top
California Angels – 45
Vic Stein – 9
Robert F. Walker/University of Arizona – 4 top left, 12, 15, 17, 24 top left, 24 bottom, 40
Viking Penguin – 11
Crandall & Assoc. – 19
Barbara Jean Germano – 18
Sports Chrome – 19, 35, 41
Mark Stewart – 48

STAFF

Project Coordinator: John Sammis, Cronopio Publishing
Series Design Concept: The Sloan Group
Design and Electronic Page Makeup: Jaffe Enterprises, and
        Digital Communications Services, Inc.

LIBRARY OF CONGRESS CATALOGING-IN-PUBLICATION DATA

Stewart, Mark.
    J. T. Snow / by Mark Stewart.
        p. cm. – (Grolier all-pro biographies)
    Includes index.
    ISBN 0-516-20170-0 (lib. binding)   0 – 516-26018-9 (pbk.)
    1. Snow, J. T. (Jack Thomas), 1968-   – Juvenile literature. 2. Baseball players–United States–
Biography–Juvenile literature. 3. California Angels (Baseball team)–Juvenile literature.
I. Title. II. Series.
865.S586S84 1996
796.357'092–dc20
(B)
                                                                        96-13038
                                                                             CIP
                                                                              AC

Grolier **ALL-PRO** *Biographies*™

J.T. Snow

by
Mark Stewart

CHILDREN'S PRESS®
A Division of Grolier Publishing
New York • London • Hong Kong • Sydney
Danbury, Connecticut

Contents

Who

Am I?

Everyone struggles at some point in life. It may be when you're a kid, or a teenager, or even when you're an adult. I always believed that when things look their darkest, you find out what kind of person you really are. When things got tough for me—when a lot of people thought I wouldn't make it—that's when I discovered that I have what it takes to succeed. My name is J. T. Snow, and this is my story . . . "

"I always believed that when things look their darkest, you find out what kind of person you really are."

Growing Up

When you are the son of a professional athlete, other people expect you to be a great athlete, too. J. T. Snow—whose father, Jack Snow, played football for the Los Angeles Rams from 1965 to 1975—lived up to those expectations. But J. T.'s path to stardom was not always an easy one. When J. T. was very young, his doctor told his parents that his legs were not developing normally. J. T.'s feet were turned in toward each other, and this condition would have to be corrected immediately.

When he was a child, J. T.'s feet were turned inward, but he outgrew this condition.

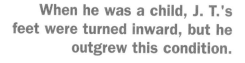

J. T. had to wear leg braces and special shoes. This made him sad, because the thing he loved most of all was playing outside with the other children in the neighborhood. It was very hard to keep up with his friends with all that equipment weighing him down. J. T.'s parents explained that someday he would not have to wear the braces anymore. And sure enough, they came off a couple of years later, and J. T.'s feet were as good as new!

The Snows lived in Seal Beach, California, a quiet community just south of Los Angeles. There was a big park in J. T.'s neighborhood where he and his friends played football and baseball. Because J. T.'s father was a famous football player, older boys would often let him play in their games. When J. T. was 10 years old, he was playing against high-school kids, and doing very well.

Although J. T. was one of the best athletes in his class, he was not one of the best students. All he could think about was how much he would like to be outside playing, which meant that sometimes he was not concentrating very hard on what the teacher was saying. English was J. T.'s most difficult subject. His spelling was excellent, but he did not always understand the rules of grammar, and sometimes he could not remember what he had read just minutes before. J. T.'s best subject was math. He could add, subtract, multiply, and divide very quickly. Whenever someone needed to compute a slugger's batting average or a quarterback's completion percentage, they could ask J. T.

"I wasn't the smartest kid in my class," J. T. recalls, "so I had to really work hard at reading. Once I got OK at it, however, I realized how important it is. Reading opened up new worlds for me. I remember the first book I ever read cover-to-cover was *Charlie and the Chocolate Factory*. It was about a boy who seemed to have very little in life, but in the end, you realized that he had a lot more than kids who got anything they wanted. As I turned the pages, I got very clear pictures in my head about what was happening and what all the characters in the book looked like and sounded like. It was a very exciting discovery for me!"

Growing up, J. T.'s favorite book was *Charlie and the Chocolate Factory.*

By the time J. T. enrolled at Los Alamitos High School, he began to think about following in his father's footsteps and becoming a professional athlete. Jack Snow had been one of the best receivers in Rams history, and after he retired he became a television broadcaster. He and his wife, Merry, encouraged J. T. to enjoy athletics, but never pushed him in any one sport. What they did insist upon was that he get his schoolwork done before he played sports. If J. T. had a practice, the rule was that he had to eat dinner and finish his homework before he could watch television. On Mondays, J. T. had to concentrate extra hard or he would miss his favorite show, "Monday Night Football."

J. T. became one of the best players on the basketball, baseball, and football teams at Los Alamitos High School. He was fast, tough, powerfully built, and had great coordination. J. T. not only earned letters in all three sports, he became one of only two athletes in history to be selected as an Orange County All-Star in each. He was captain of the basketball team as a junior, and he captained all three teams in his senior year.

All of J. T.'s friends assumed that he would carry on the family tradition and be a football player. In fact, the college his father attended, Notre Dame University, offered J. T. a football scholarship. But Notre Dame's coach, Lou Holtz, wanted J. T. to play defensive back, and J. T. wanted to play on offense. He did not think he would be happy playing a position he did not like, so he declined Notre Dame's offer.

When J. T. realized that no other major university wanted him as its quarterback, he sat down with his mother and father to discuss his future. His favorite sport was basketball, but all three agreed that, at 6' 2", he was not tall enough to make it all the way to the NBA. Being left-handed, his chances of becoming an NFL quarterback would also be very poor. So J. T. and his parents decided he should concentrate on baseball. It was not his favorite sport, but everything from his size to his skill as a switch-hitter suggested that baseball would be the smartest choice.

The only problem was that few colleges had bothered to scout J. T. as a baseball player because they assumed he would choose football or basketball. Luckily, a coach from the University of Arizona recommended that the school offer him a scholarship. The coach had never seen J. T. play baseball, but he had attended a football game during which J. T. was sacked several times. He had admired J. T.'s toughness and determination. Any kid who can put up with that, he told Merry Snow, can play baseball for us!

J. T. decided to attend the University of Arizona on a baseball scholarship.

College

J. T. Snow arrived on the University of Arizona campus in the fall of 1986 as a ballplayer first, and as a student second. That did not mean he intended to neglect his studies. J. T. knew that the odds of making it to the majors were against him, so he decided to take courses that would give him a well-rounded education if he did not succeed as a professional baseball player. His favorite class was public speaking, where he learned how to give speeches to groups of people. "The best class I ever took was that public speaking class. I actually had to get up in front of people and give speeches. That really helped me. In my profession, being able to express myself clearly is important, and I like being able to stand in front of a crowd without being afraid or scared. That really helps when I have to give a talk to kids. They can be the scariest audience of all!"

Years

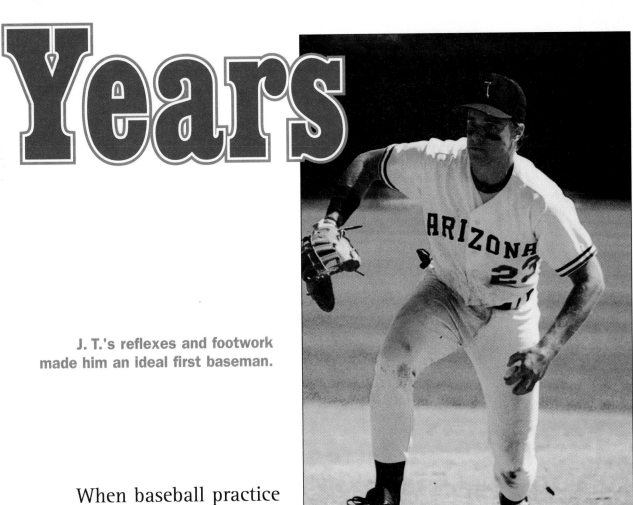

J. T.'s reflexes and footwork made him an ideal first baseman.

When baseball practice started, J. T. was told he would play first base. The soft hands, quick reflexes, and footwork he had developed in basketball and football made him perfect for the position. That was fine with him—he had played the position in high school.

Trevor Hoffman (left) and Scott Erickson (right) were two pitching stars on J. T.'s college team who also succeeded in the major leagues.

J. T.'s three seasons with the Arizona Wildcats were good ones, but he was far from the best player on the team. That honor went to pitchers Trevor Hoffman and Scott Erickson. Both went on to achieve success in the major leagues. Hoffman became an ace reliever, and Erickson pitched a no-hitter for the Minnesota Twins.

In 1989, everything came together for the Arizona Wildcats, and they won the PAC 10 conference championship. It was also J. T.'s breakthrough season. He batted .359 and led the conference with an on-base percentage of .470. That meant he reached base nearly half the times he came to the plate! He was most pleased with his consistency in batting from both sides of the plate; he hit .360 as a lefty and .351 as a righty in 1989.

J. T. Snow's college baseball statistics:

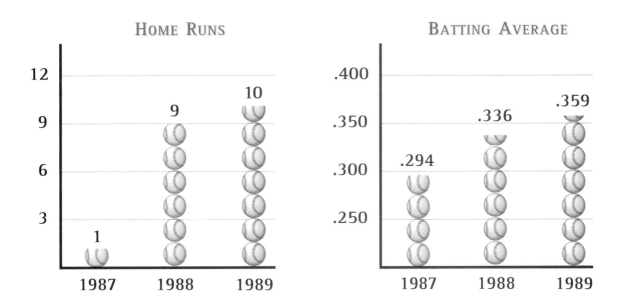

Home Runs

Year	Home Runs
1987	1
1988	9
1989	10

Batting Average

Year	Batting Average
1987	.294
1988	.336
1989	.359

When J. T. heard that he had been drafted by the New York Yankees, he made the decision to leave college and become a professional baseball player.

J. T. beats the throw and steals second.

The Story

The New York Yankees selected J. T. Snow in the fifth round of the 1989 draft. They hoped that he would some day be good enough to replace Don Mattingly, their major-league first baseman, whose career was beginning to slow down. J. T. rewarded the team's confidence in him by batting .292 in his first minor-league season, and leading the league in fielding average. So began a quick rise through the Yankee farm system. In 1992, J. T. earned a share of the International League batting title and was chosen as the league's MVP. As a reward for his remarkable progress, the Yankees called him up to the majors for the final two weeks of the 1992 season.

J. T. had his best minor-league year with the Columbus Clippers.

18

Continues

Yankee fans hoped J. T. would succeed
Don Mattingly as the team's first baseman.

J. T. was excited about playing for the Yankees in 1993. He looked forward to learning from Don Mattingly, who was one of the American League's best first basemen, both in the field and at the plate. But just two months after the season ended, J. T. received the shocking news that he had been traded. The Yankees had packaged J. T. along with two young pitchers and sent the trio to the Angels in exchange for pitcher Jim Abbott. That was the bad news. The good news was that J. T. would be playing in Anaheim, California— just 20 minutes from where he grew up. And he would be given every chance to become the team's regular first baseman. Angels fans were not happy about losing Abbott, but they were very happy to receive a highly rated hometown hero in return.

Pitcher Jim Abbott came to the Yankees in the trade that sent J. T. to California.

J. T.'s first season with the Angels started wonderfully. In his first 63 at bats, he had 6 home runs and 17 RBIs, and his batting average was .343. But that power surge ended up hurting J. T., who started swinging for homers on pitches he would normally have driven for singles and doubles. His average quickly plummeted, and before he knew it, he was back in the minors.

"When I started so well in 1993, I began to think this game was easy. I thought I could hit anything. That was a mistake. Pitchers made adjustments and I started to get myself out. Then I got down on myself, and to make up for it, I'd try to do too much. I was trying to make things happen instead of relaxing and letting things happen. After I went to the minors, I learned that my goal should be to play nine hard innings and be happy with that."

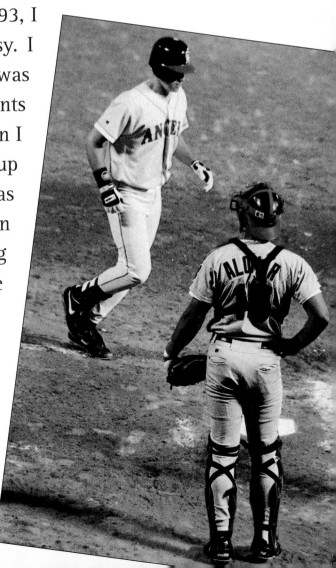

J. T. crosses the plate after hitting his second home run of an April 1993 game.

J. T. played his way back to the major leagues in 1994, and by the end of the season he had won the starting first-base job again. As the 1995 season opened, everyone in baseball knew it was J. T.'s "do-or-die" season. Could he struggle back from adversity and become the player everyone had predicted, or would he continue his inconsistent play?

J. T. started strong in 1995 and finished even stronger. Pitchers could no longer make him swing at balls out of the strike zone, which meant they had to give him something good to hit. And when they did, J. T. connected. He launched 24 homers and knocked in 102 runs. His batting average zoomed to .289—69 points higher than the year before! In the field, J. T. won the Gold Glove award for his great defensive performance at first base.

Now J. T. Snow is an established star with an exciting, young team. And he should be among the best in the business for many years to come.

The California Angels improved right along with J. T. In 1994, the team had finished 32 games out of first place. In 1995, they ended the season tied for the AL West lead.

In 1995, pitchers were giving J. T. nothing good to hit.
Still, J. T. slugged 24 homers.

Timeline

1987: Starts at first base for Arizona Wildcats

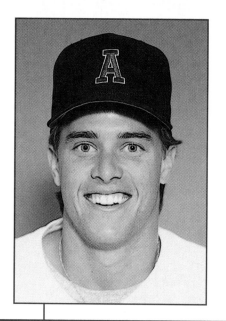

1992: Makes major-league debut with New York Yankees

1989: Bats .359 for Wildcats and earns All-PAC 10 honors

**1993: Joins
California
Angels**

**1995: Leads
Angels to tie
for Western
Division
crown**

Game

J. T. is proud of his offensive contributions. "Sometimes my bat tends to get overlooked because people seem to notice my defense more."

J. T.'s offensive contributions include being a smart base runner.

J. T. wore number 6 in the minors and wears it now. "I like single-digit uniform numbers," he says.

Action!

J. T. hit a home run in his first game as a California Angel on April 6, 1993.

Nothing makes J. T. feel better than scooping up a ball to help a teammate. "Saving an error and saving a base runner, that's my job."

J. T. doesn't like the spotlight. "I'd rather be the guy who quietly goes about his business and then you look up and say, 'Hey, he's having a good year.'"

J. T.'s major-league debut was a seven-game stint with the Yankees at the end of the 1992 season. He got two hits and two RBIs during his brief stay in New York.

J. T. is one of only six American League first basemen who have won a Gold Glove and driven in 100 runs in the same season. The last to do it was his former teammate with the Yankees, Don Mattingly.

After making a spectacular diving catch, J. T. throws from his knees.

J. T. credits Angels batting coach Rod Carew with helping him stay focused at the plate. Carew was one of the greatest hitters in baseball history. His career batting average was .328.

J. T. and hitting coach Rod Carew work on a one-handed hitting drill.

"Being a switch-hitter, I have to work very hard on hitting right-handed, because it's not my natural side. I am naturally left-handed."

J. T. did some timely hitting in 1995. His clutch hits delivered RBIs that gave the Angels a lead 15 times and tied a game 8 other times.

J. T. is congratulated by teammate
Chili Davis after a 1995 home run.

Dealing

California Angels fans were thrilled with J. T. Snow at the beginning of the 1993 season. He batted .343 in April and looked more like an All-Star than a rookie. But from May to July he hit just .188, and the cheers turned to boos. Eventually, the Angels sent him back to the minors. Most players never recover from this kind of embarrassment, but for J. T. it was his wake-up call.

"I stepped back and asked myself why I was successful in the beginning. I got back to being patient at the plate and hitting my pitches. I batted .340 the rest of that season in the minors and won back the starting job the following year. The hardest thing is to keep those doubts from creeping in . . . you just have to fight them off."

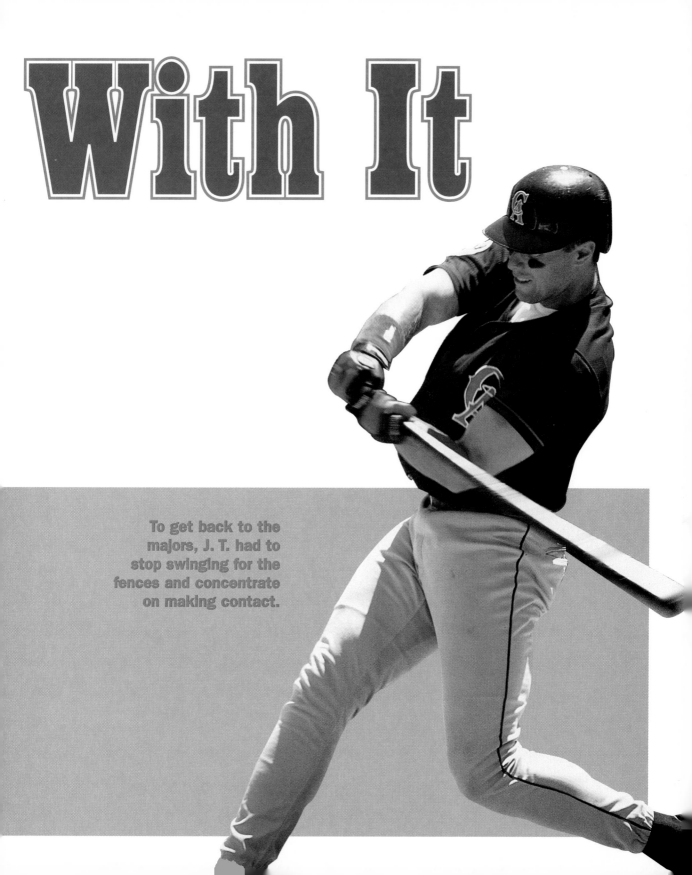

With It

To get back to the majors, J. T. had to stop swinging for the fences and concentrate on making contact.

How Does

J. T. Snow was not born a great fielder. He has worked for years to improve his defense. When he was young, his father would hit him a bucket of balls. If J. T. missed one, his father would refill the bucket and start again. They would not go home until he had fielded every ball perfectly. J. T. still takes hundreds of grounders a week—a routine that earned him the Gold Glove in 1995.

"It takes good hands and good feet to play first base. Even if your infielder makes a bad throw, it's still the first baseman's job to catch it."

J. T. has to be ready for any throw.

He Do It?

J. T. fields hundreds of balls during practice.

Family

J. T. and Stacie Snow were married in 1993. They are planning to have children someday, but for now they have all they can handle with their two dogs. J. T. remains close to his parents and his sisters, Michelle and Stephanie. Because J. T.'s dad is a broadcaster in the Los Angeles area, they are able to see each other often.

J. T. and Stacie work together at local schools in a program that encourages kids to read. When J. T. talks—or reads—children listen.

"Any time I can help kids out, I try to make the time. They get a real kick out of having a ballplayer come to see them, and that makes me feel really good, like I'm making a difference."

Matters

J. T. and his father, Jack Snow

Say What?

Here's what people are saying about J. T. Snow:

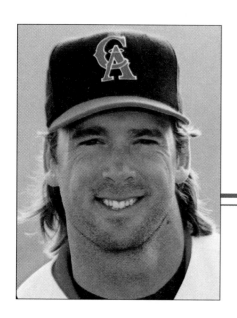

"I'd hate to take J. T. off first base. He's saved a lot of rear ends over there."

—*Chuck Finley, teammate*

"He's not a power hitter, he's a gap hitter."

—*Rod Carew, Angels hitting coach*

"You feel so comfortable with J. T. It's like no matter where you throw it, he's going to make a great play."

—*Torey Lovullo, former teammate*

"He's as good as Don Mattingly defensively."

—*Mark Langston, teammate*

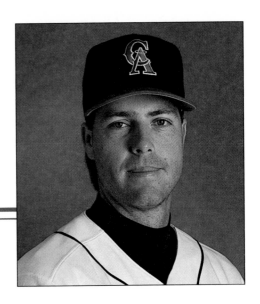

"I didn't push J. T. into baseball. I told him whatever sport you choose, make up your mind and be the best at it."

—*Jack Snow, J. T.'s father*

"A lot of people gave up on him. That created a lot of pressure on him to produce. You want to see people do well in those circumstances."

—*Tim Salmon, teammate*

Career

J. T. holds down first for the Arizona Wildcats.

With a few more years like his 1995 season, J. T. Snow could establish himself as the top all-around first baseman in the American League. His glovework leaves little room for improvement, and he is already one of the top switch-hitters in the game. Just watching him in action, however, makes you believe the best is yet to come.

Highlights

J. T. earned All-PAC 10 honors in 1989 as the conference's top first baseman.

J. T.'s glove has always been a potent weapon. In fact, he was a three-time fielding champion in the minor leagues.

J. T.'s minor-league average of .313 in 1992 earned him a tie for the International League batting title.

J. T. was named International League MVP and Rookie of the Year in 1992.

J. T. is the Angels' main man at first base.

J. T. hits for average and power from both sides of the plate.

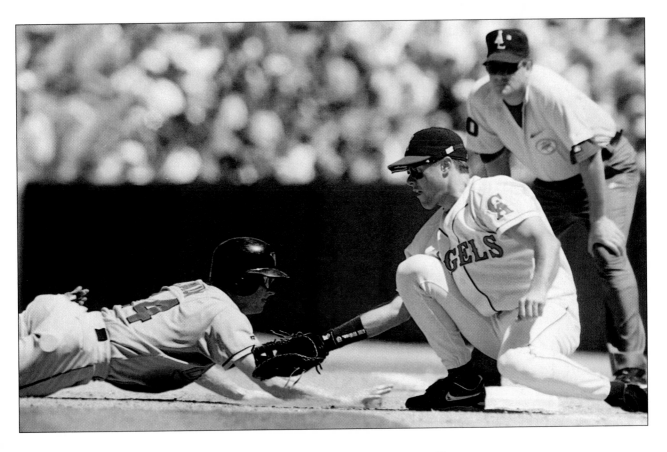

J. T. attempts to pick off Baltimore Orioles runner Greg Zaun.

J. T. led major-league switch-hitters with 102 RBIs in 1995. He was fifth among switch-hitters in home runs.

J. T. won the Gold Glove in 1995 as the AL's top-fielding first baseman in 1995. His former teammate, Don Mattingly, had won the award from 1991 to 1994.

Numbers

Name: Jack Thomas Snow Jr.

Born: February 26, 1968

Height: 6' 2"

Weight: 205 pounds

Uniform Number: 6

College: University of Arizona

J. T. has already established himself as the best switch-hitting infielder in California Angels history.

Year	Team	Games	At Bats	Hits	Home Runs	Runs	RBIs	Batting Average	Fielding Average
1992	New York Yankees	7	14	2	0	1	2	.143	1.000
1993	California Angels	129	419	101	16	60	57	.241	.995
1994	California Angels	61	223	49	8	22	30	.220	.996
1995	California Angels	143	544	157	24	80	102	.289	.997
TOTALS		340	1,200	309	48	163	191	.258	.996

Glossary

ADVERSITY misfortune; trouble; calamity

CONSISTENCY steady continuity; regularity of quality

DECLINED turned down; said no

EVALUATE to determine worth or value by careful appraisal and study

INCONSISTENT changeable; up and down; erratic

PLUMMET to fall sharply and quickly

PREDICT to guess what will happen in the future

SCHOLARSHIP money given to a student to help pay for schooling

SOFT HANDS a sports term used to describe the ability to catch balls effortlessly, without tensing the hands

Index

About The Author

Mark Stewart grew up in New York City in the 1960s and 1970s– when the Mets, Jets, and Knicks all had championship teams. As a child, Mark read everything about sports he could lay his hands on. Today, he is one of the busiest sportswriters around. Since 1990, he has written close to 500 sports stories for kids, including profiles on more than 200 athletes, past and present. A graduate of Duke University, Mark served as senior editor of *Racquet*, a national tennis magazine, and was managing editor of *Super News*, a sporting goods industry newspaper. He is the author of every Grolier All-Pro Biography.

DATE DUE

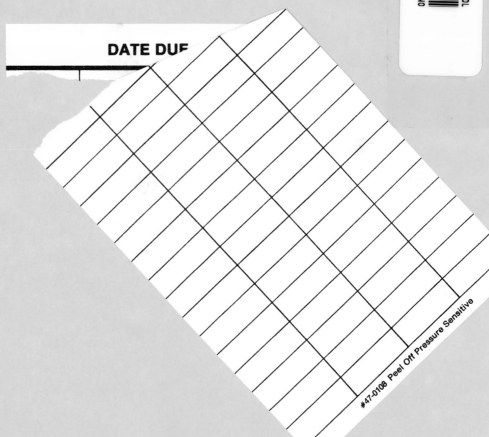

#47-0108 Peel Off Pressure Sensitive